The Indo-Pac

India's Maritime Highway to Great Power Status

39th USI NATIONAL SECURITY PAPER 2023

The Indo-Pacific Construct
India's Maritime Highway to Great Power Status

Vice Admiral Anil Kumar Chawla, PVSM, AVSM, NM, VSM, PhD (Retd)

(Established 1870)

United Service Institution of India

New Delhi (India)

Vij Books
New Delhi (India)

Published by

Vij Books
(Publishers, Distributors & Importers)
4836/24, Ansari Road
Delhi - 110 002
Phones: 91-11-43596460
Mob: 98110 94883
e-mail: contact@vijpublishing.com
web : www.vijbooks.in

First Published in India in 2024

ISBN: 978-81-19438-55-6

Contents

The Indo-Pacific Construct India's Maritime Highway to Great Power Status

> *"Whosoever commands the sea commands the trade of the world, commands the riches of the world, and consequently the world itself".*
>
> **—Sir Walter Raleigh, 1616**

Introduction

The Indo-Pacific has emerged as the pre-eminent geopolitical and geo-economic construct in the second decade of the 21st century, replacing the post-cold war Asia-Pacific formulation. This has been driven by two main reasons: the economic and demographic vitality of the region and the emergence of a non-democratic and aggressive China as a global maritime power with its strategic sights set firmly on dominating the Indian and Pacific oceans. China's attempt to disrupt and disregard the existing global rule-based order, as shown by its behaviour in the South China and East China Seas, could be a precursor to such behaviour elsewhere. This has led to the coalescing of interests between the major democratic powers in the region, reflected most prominently in the Quadrilateral Security Dialogue (QUAD) grouping comprising Australia, India, Japan and the United States (US).

It is happenstance that the coming into being of the Indo-Pacific construct has coincided with India's emergence as a major economic, scientific and cultural power, with a demographic dividend to boot. As the most populous nation in the world, India has rightful ambitions to take its place in the vanguard of the comity of nations. The government has also recently announced the target of making India a developed nation by 2047, the centenary of our independence.

There has always been an organic connection between maritime power and a country achieving 'Great Power' status. Maritime power, however, remains a weak link in the elements comprising India's Comprehensive National Power (CNP). This paper argues that the Indo-Pacific construct offers India an opportune avenue to rejuvenate its maritime power and expand its influence, especially in the western end of the construct, the Indian Ocean Region (IOR), which would be a vital enabler for India's emergence as a developed nation by 2047, and its eventual rise as a 'Great Power'.

The Organic Connection between Maritime Power and 'Great Power' Status

Historically, maritime strength has been a pre-requisite for any power to maximise its CNP. All great civilisations, the Indian, Phoenician, Greek, Roman and Chinese, had substantial maritime capability, both military and mercantile. This enabled overseas conquests, facilitated trade and economic growth, and spread of their cultural, religious and civilisational influence across the world. Notable examples include the Roman conquest of Egypt and Britain between 30 BCE and 87 CE, the spread of Hinduism and Buddhism from India to Southeast and East Asia commencing around 300 BCE and the colonisation of large parts of Asia, Africa and the US by European maritime powers between the 15th and 19th centuries. Indeed, history clearly demonstrates that the oceans were a strategic highway and a medium by which one group of people could dominate the affairs of another. The Portuguese colonial empire was an especially good example of a 'Thalassocracy', an empire founded on mastery of the sea. While their soldiers were never sufficiently numerous to engage in major continental campaigns, their 160-year empire in the Indian Ocean rested on a few garrisons in strategic locations and on superior naval forces.

As trade and manufacturing developed, there was a need for countries to establish a degree of control over not just resources, but also markets in which to sell their products. This was the genesis of dedicated navies, which gave the country possessing them three major advantages: security from invasion across the oceans; mobility and capacity to reach the enemy's shores; and freedom to travel and trade across the seas. Some sea powers, such as Great Britain, also formulated a grand plan to use the seas, along with the other tangible and intangible resources, they had at their disposal, to enhance and protect their interests, understood today as a 'Maritime Strategy'.

Sea power has two aspects to it, which are closely related: military power on the one hand and commercial maritime power on the other, which derives from sea-borne trade, the fishing industry, ship-building, etc. Maritime strategy, therefore, may be seen as a much broader, more flexible and ultimately more effective source of national power, prosperity and success than its land or air equivalents. However, a maritime strategy needs to be intelligently conceived and applied by states if they aim to take optimum advantage of their positions.[1] It is also evident that sea power has been more closely connected with the socio-economic development of mankind than has been either land or air power. Maritime strategy is also a more versatile and effective instrument of national power, prosperity and success than its land or air equivalents. It is, therefore, not surprising that sea power has been critical for the economic, social and territorial security of countries. Its presence has enabled their rise, and its absence has contributed greatly to their downfall.

The organic connection between sea power and 'Great Power' status was first highlighted in a comprehensive manner by Alfred Thayer Mahan. In his seminal work, '*The Influence of Sea Power upon History: 1660 to 1783*', Mahan argued that sea power tipped the strategic initiative in favour of the state that exercised it better. He posited, "Twice has there been witnessed the struggle of the highest individual genius against the resources and institutions of a great nation, and in both cases the nation was victorious. For seventeen years Hannibal strove against Rome, for sixteen years Napoleon strove against England; the efforts of the first ended in Zama, those of the second in Waterloo in both cases, the mastery of the sea rested with the victor".[2]

If we take the pre-eminent colonial power, Great Britain as a case study, the contribution of maritime power to make Britain 'Great' is clearly evident. Its strategists understood that control of the oceans assured control of the land. Losing them would result in an imperial decline. The security of their empire then rested on a series of defensive and offensive strategies centred on controlling the sea.[3] Of course, maritime power was not the only element that went into making it a 'Great Power'. Its geographical insulation from the continent of Europe, with the English Channel acting as a great moat, was a key factor. The separation of state and the church in the 13th century, the Age of Enlightenment in the 15th century and the industrial revolution in the 18th century, were other factors that made Great Britain the world's uncontested scientific and technological power and also the world's factory. The resulting prosperity led to an outward expansion to find new markets (colonies) and protect its overseas trade, which in turn spurred the development of a world-class navy. Indeed, the Royal Navy was the fulcrum on which the British colonial empire was established and supported, which, at its zenith, encompassed 25 percent of the globe, over which it was famously stated, "The sun never sets". This, in turn, brought vast natural and human resources under their sway, as also captive markets for their products, with a virtuous cycle of unimpeded economic growth, and the easy availability of funds for military and naval development. The two century-long reign of Great Britain from the early 18th to the early 20th centuries ended when its strength was sapped by two world wars and its economy was denuded by the independence of its colonies, especially India.

The case of China, a continental power that briefly established global maritime links, offers a contrarian example to Great Britain to prove the fact that being a maritime power and achieving a 'Great Power' status are closely inter-connected. China had built a society of great scientific and economic sophistication in the period preceding and up to the 15th century, and its maritime power also rose to its zenith during the early Ming Empire. During this period the Chinese achieved major advances in ship-building and navigation, such as double hulls and transverse bulkheads with separate watertight compartments, which enabled better seaworthiness and the building of larger ships; as also magnetic compass and star charts for astronavigation. From 1405 to 1433 the Yongle (Ming) Emperor's eunuch Admiral Zheng led seven ocean expeditions to Southeast Asia, India and East Africa with hundreds of ships comprising his fleet (he died at sea in 1433). Some of the larger ships, dubbed as 'Treasure ships' were over 400 feet long with nine masts and four decks, a size that would only be achieved again in the 19th century. These ships could carry 2,500 tons of cargo and were armed with small cannons.

However, Ming China withdrew from the seas in a deliberate move for three main reasons. The first was the demise of the main sponsor of the voyages, the Yongle Emperor in 1424, and the assumption of the throne of his son, the Hongxi Emperor, who was much more conservative and Confucianist in his thought. Secondly, the treasure fleets cost the Ming Empire enormous amounts of money, and since they were not trade excursions, China recovered little of the cost. Thirdly, recurrent threats from Central Asia and several natural disasters sapped the strength of the Ming Empire, forcing them to concentrate their attention on their land borders. So, in 1477, when another seafaring expedition was proposed, the Hongxi Emperor was persuaded by the Minister of War to order the destruction of all Zheng He's records in the archives and a decree was passed banning the construction of any ship with more than two masts, as also the destruction of all ocean-going ships. By 1525, possibly, one of the largest navies in history, once comprising 3,500 ships, was gone. When the Portuguese landed in southern China in 1513, the absence of Chinese maritime power enabled them to quickly establish a firm foot-hold. This was later emulated by other European maritime powers and Japan, leading to the subjugation of a once powerful empire.

The successor of 'Great Power' status to Great Britain was the US. US maritime power, which developed commencing the beginning of the 20th century, peaked during the Second World War and enabled its ascent to 'Great Power' status in the early 20th century. The US remains the globe's primary maritime military power and a 'Great Power' till today, though its predominance in non-military maritime power has been long overtaken by Japan, South Korea, and now China. In its quest to achieve 'Great Power' status, China has assiduously developed its maritime power over the last four decades to emerge as the primary maritime challenger to the US.

Figure 1 below illustrates the global share of Gross Domestic Product (GDP) of major world powers over the past 2,000 years. While the GDP of each country depends on a number of factors, such as population, geographic extent and location, industrialisation, governance, etc. there is an evident strong correlation between maritime power and economic growth over the past two millennia. If we take India as an example, its share of global GDP was the largest around 1 CE. It started reducing gradually as invasions from Central Asia sapped India's vitality and also diverted its attention from the seas towards the land. Similar patterns are also visible with the United Kingdom (UK), the US and China.

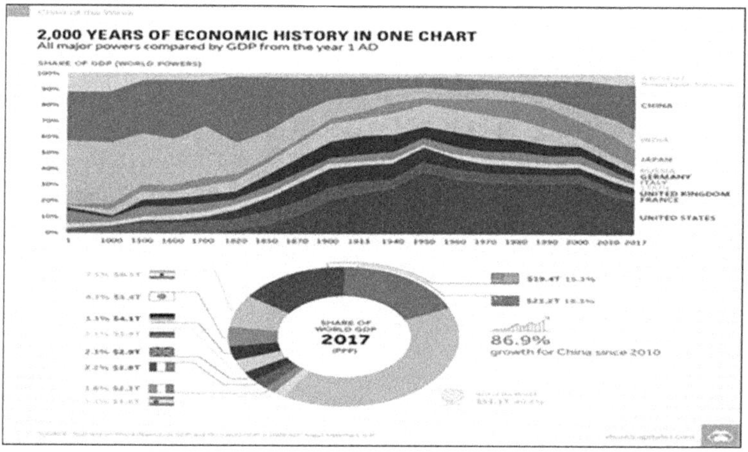

Figure 1 - Economic History of the Last 2,000 years in one Graph[4]

Mackinder's and Spykman's Theories

The superiority of sea power over continental power is underlined by the geopolitical theories of Mackinder and Spykman. Sir Halford Mackinder, a well-known political geographer from Great Britain, postulated 'Mackinder's Theory' in 1904. The theory proposed that whoever controlled Eastern Europe, would control the 'Heartland', which comprised Central Asia, the high seas around it and Eurasia. Whoever controlled the 'Heartland' would control the 'World Island' and rule the world.[5] The theory was supposedly a major reason behind Nazi Germany's disastrous invasion of the Soviet Union in 1940. The theory seems to have also been adopted by the Soviet Union during the Cold War, as they amassed Soviet Republics in Central Asia and dropped the 'Iron Curtain' over Eastern Europe.

Nichols Spykman, an American political geographer, countered Mackinder's Heartland Theory in 1942 by proposing 'Spykman's Theory'.[6] This theory stated that Eurasia's 'Rimland', i.e., its coastal areas, were the key to controlling the 'World Island'. Spykman proposed that, the 'Rimland' contained the 'Heartland'. Whoever controlled the 'Rimland' would control the 'World Island' and eventually the world. Spykman's Theory was proved correct, both in the Second World War, and in the Cold War, when the continental powers, Germany and the Soviet Union, were defeated by the allied powers and the west respectively, using maritime power as the principal fulcrum for force application. As Spykman stated with regard to the Cold War, 'By enlisting the Rimland countries against the Soviets, by using central Europe as a bridgehead, Great Britain as an unsinkable aircraft carrier and Canada and the US as resource bases for material and manpower, they denied the Soviets access to the sea and ultimately won the Cold War'. In today's scenario, Spykman's theory seems to resonate once again in the form of the Indo-Pacific construct, as later paragraphs will show.

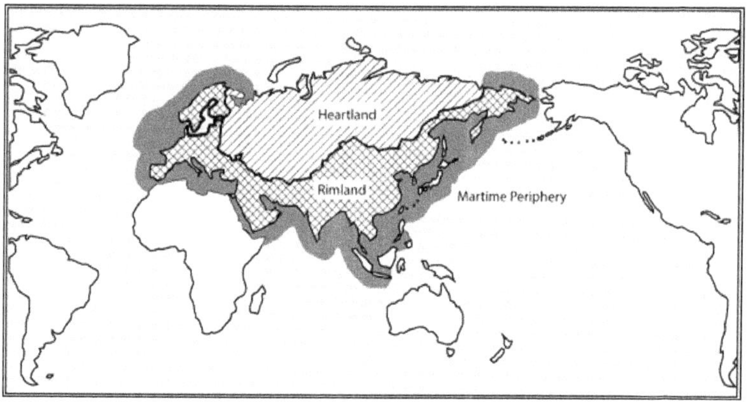

Figure 2 - Mackinder's Heartland and Spykman's Rimland[7]

Evolution of the Indo-Pacific Construct

Traditionally, any grouping of countries, geographical regions or entities is founded on some homogeneity, either of origin or of purpose. The homogeneity could be based on geographic, oceanographic, geopolitical, geostrategic, geo-economic, security-related, cultural, linguistic, ethnic, civilisational, biogeographic, climatological or environmental factors. When one or more of these factors overlap, the grouping becomes stronger. The examples of the North Atlantic Treaty Organisation, Group of Seven (G-7) and the European Union (EU) are classic examples of groupings with multiple commonalities, and hence greater resilience and unity of purpose.

While the Indo-Pacific region may seem to be too vast for any homogeneity, as the Indian and the Pacific Oceans, together encompass over 50 percent of the earth's surface (excluding the land masses of their littorals),[8] from a maritime geography point of view, the Indian and Pacific Oceans can be seen as 'Conjoined Oceans', connected by the umbilical of Southeast Asia. Consequently, there has always been greater biogeographic, oceanographic, climatological and civilisational interplay between the Indian and Pacific Oceans, as compared to the Atlantic region, where the barriers imposed by the continental land masses of the

Americas and Africa, have reduced this substantially. Examples of this close interaction include the similarity and richness of ocean species in the Indo-Pacific region and climatological phenomena such as the El Nino/La Nina Southern Oscillation in central and eastern equatorial Pacific,[9] which is closely linked with the development of monsoons in the Indian Ocean, and directly impacts the lives of people on the Indian sub-continent. The various straits that link the Indian and Pacific Oceans have also facilitated maritime interaction between the two oceans since ancient times, exemplified by the spread of Buddhism in Southeast and East Asia from ancient India, as far east as Japan.

The earliest espousal of the Indo-Pacific as a distinct region stems from Weimar Germany's concept of an anti-colonial India and Republican China as German allies against Euro-America,[10] described in detail in German political oceanographer Karl Hausopher's work, 'Indopazifischen Raum' (Indo-Pacific region), written in the 1920s. In the 21st century, the coming into vogue of the term 'Indo-Pacific' has been first ascribed to the Japanese Prime Minister's address to the Indian Parliament in Aug 2007, titled 'Confluence of the Two Seas', where he referred to the 'Dynamic coupling between the Indian and Pacific Oceans as seas of freedom and prosperity'.[11] This address was preceded by a paper published by the Institute of Defence Studies and Analyses in Jan 2007 in collaboration with the Japan Institute of International Affairs.[12]

The term gained traction in the West in the 2010s, and the Trump administration included the Indo-Pacific construct in the US National Security Strategy released in Dec 2017, defining the region as 'Stretching from the west coast of India to the western shores of the United States', with four priority action areas: political; economic; and military and security.[13] In May 2018, the US also renamed its largest and oldest combatant command, the Pacific Command (PACOM), as the Indo-Pacific Command, though the geographical boundary in the Indian Ocean has been retained at 68 degrees East, as was the case with the PACOM. This excludes the western Indian Ocean from its area of responsibility, and divides it between the US Central Command and the US

Africa Command. The latest document promulgated by the Biden Administration on 11 Feb 2022 is the 'Indo-Pacific Strategy', which envisions the Indo-Pacific region as encompassing 'Northeast Asia and Southeast Asia, to South Asia and Oceania, including the Pacific Islands'.[14] Interestingly, the US strategy also mentions the Euro-Atlantic as a complementary region to the Indo-Pacific.

All major powers (except China and Russia) have accepted the Indo-Pacific concept. Japan's plan for a 'Free and Open Indo-Pacific' was unveiled in 2016 and updated in Mar 2023. In May 2018, the French President set out the French strategy for the Indo-Pacific region, which was formally promulgated as a policy document in Feb 2022.[15] Australia's vision for a 'Free and Open' Indo-Pacific and Association of South East Asian Nation (ASEAN) Outlook to the Indo-Pacific were both released in 2019. Germany also promulgated a set of 'Guidelines on the Indo-Pacific' in Sep 2020.[16] The EU promulgated its 'Strategy for Cooperation in the Indo-Pacific' on 16 Sep 2021 and defined the region as 'Spanning from the east coast of Africa to the Pacific Island States'.[17] Canada's Indo-Pacific strategy was promulgated in 2022, and Indian Ocean Rim Association's Indo-Pacific Outlook in 2023. Many other smaller countries have also issued policy documents on the Indo-Pacific concept, signalling its wide acceptance.

India considers the Indo-Pacific as extending from the eastern shores of Africa to the western shores of America. India's vision of the Indo-Pacific, as outlined by Prime Minister Modi at the Shangri La Dialogue in Singapore in 2018, envisages a 'Free, open, inclusive, peaceful, and prosperous Indo-Pacific region built on a rule-based international order, sustainable and transparent infrastructure investment, freedom of navigation and over-flight, unimpeded lawful commerce, mutual respect for sovereignty, peaceful resolution of disputes, as well as equality of all nations'.[18] India supports all endeavours to advance its vision, including initiatives to enhance trade, connectivity, people-to-people interaction and cultural connections between Indo-Pacific countries.

China's Maritime Rise and the 'Two-Ocean' Concept

While the Indo-Pacific concept has been consistently opposed by China, what is not very commonly known is that a variation of the Indo-Pacific formulation was adopted by China in 2004, though under a different name i.e., the 'Two-Ocean' strategy. China's reorientation towards the seas, which commenced in the early 1980s (coinciding with its economic opening up to the world), was fundamentally fed by the realisation that it could not become a 'Great Power' unless it was also a maritime power. An exponential increase in dependence on maritime trade and other sea-borne activities and depletion of its land-based resources was another reason - China has been a net importer of food and energy since 1993 and by 2035, it is expected to import 80 percent of its oil and 46 percent of its natural gas. Reorientation towards the seas has increased China's share of global GDP from 2.26 percent in 1980 to 18.92 percent in 2023, which is projected to reach 20 percent in 2030.[19] In 1976, China was ranked 34th in global exports with a global share of 0.69 percent; in 2022, this had reached to 14.4 percent. Indeed, China has been the largest exporter of goods in the world since 2009.

China's 2004 Defence White Paper announced a major shift in its maritime strategy from 'Near seas defence' to 'Far seas operations' with the long-term aim of achieving the 'Command of the seas'.[20] The Two-Ocean strategy began to appear in Chinese literature as a pre-conceptualised project of the Communist Party of China from 2005.[21] The strategy was expanded in the '*Science of Military Strategy (2013)*',[22] an important policy document published by China's Academy of Military Sciences (since updated in the 2020 edition). The document stated that China's national interests had 'Surpassed the traditional territorial land, territorial sea and territorial air space to continuously expand towards the periphery and the world, extending towards the ocean, space and electromagnetic space'. It went on to state that 'The main war threat had switched from the traditional inland direction towards the ocean direction', the People's Liberation Army (PLA) 'Must expand its military strategic view and provide strong and strategic support within a greater spatial scope to maintain national interests'.[23] The document described the Two-Ocean region as 'Mainly including the Pacific Ocean, Indian Ocean, as well as the littoral regions of neighbouring Asia, Africa, Oceania, North America, South America and Antarctica, spanning 50 percent of the globe and 71 percent of the global ocean area'.[24] It deemed the Two-Ocean region extremely important for China's security interests, representing 'A crucial area in influencing China's strategic development and security in the future, as well as the intermediate zone of entrance into the Mediterranean Sea and Arctic region'.

China has developed its military and non-military maritime power in consonance with the broad requirements of the Two-Ocean concept. Its unprecedented naval modernisation has made it the largest naval force in the world and the second most powerful after the US Navy, not counting its expanding coast guard and maritime militia. China also has the largest merchant shipping fleet in the world (combined with Hong Kong and Macau), and is the second largest ship-builder, after South Korea. It has one of the largest ocean and polar research programmes in the world. Seven of the ten busiest ports in the world are in China. China's fishing fleet is by far the world's largest, with over 5,64,000 ocean-going vessels. It is not surprising that the seaward leg of the Belt and Road Initiative (BRI), the Maritime silk route lies entirely within the 'Two-Ocean' region described in the 'Science of Military Strategy (2013)'.

Contrasting Visions of the Indo-Pacific

From the foregoing, it is evident that while the geographical expanse of the Indo-Pacific region is broadly the same between China, the West and India, their strategic visions are very different. The US frames its vision in terms of five objectives: advance a free and open Indo-Pacific; build connections within and outside the region; drive regional prosperity; bolster Indo-Pacific security; and build resilience to transnational threats. The EU strategy has outlined seven priority areas, largely similar to the objectives listed by the US: sustainable and inclusive prosperity; green transition; ocean governance; digital governance and partnerships; connectivity; security and defence; and human security.[25] It is also evident that both the US and the EU strategies are aimed, at either countering or containing China. The US strategy states that, 'The intensifying American focus is due in part to the fact that the Indo-Pacific faces mounting challenges, particularly from the People's Republic of China (PRC). The PRC is combining its economic, diplomatic, and technological might as it pursues a sphere of influence in the Indo-Pacific and seeks to become the world's most influential power'.[26] While the EU Strategy for the Indo-Pacific is more guarded in naming China, the emphasis on an open and rules based regional security architecture leaves no room for doubt about who it is designed against. Both the US and the EU strategy formulations can, therefore, be seen as geopolitical and geo-economic counters to China's Two-Ocean strategy. India's vision on the other hand emphasises the inclusive and peaceful use of the Indo-Pacific region built on a rule-based international order, and also implicitly calls out China for its aggressive actions in the South China Sea. In that sense, it is broadly congruent with the US and EU strategies.

While the western formulation and India's Indo-Pacific vision frames a future Indo-Pacific in terms of a multilateral, inclusive and democratic region, China's Two-Ocean strategy looks at the area purely from the perspective of its own national security and economic prosperity. As stated in the *Science of Military Strategy (2013)*, it wants Chinese actors to: 'Create conditions to establish ourselves in the Two-Ocean region, participate in resource extraction and space utilisation of the oceans, and boost development in the two Polar Regions'. The document expects traditional and non-traditional 'Security Threats' to oppose this sweeping geostrategic expansion,[27] thereby building a rationale for further concerted qualitative and quantitative development of their armed forces, especially their Navy.[28] The Two-Ocean strategy is a sub-set of China's Grand Strategy to supplant the US as the premier world power by 2049, the year the PRC completes its centenary of formation. As part of this strategy, China seeks to build a set of client states across the region, which would be partially or wholly dependent on China. However, its unilateral approach, which stems from its 'Middle Kingdom' complex, is inherently flawed. The absence of any homogeneity, other than dependence on China, can never be the basis for a strong alliance, certainly not one required to dominate a region as vast and diverse as the Indo-Pacific. The example of the US, which has been the leading power in the Indo-Pacific since the end of World War II, in alliance with like-minded treaty partners such as Japan, South Korea and Australia, as also major defence partners such as India, amply illustrates this reality.

Strategic Significance of the Indo-Pacific

The geostrategic importance of the Indo-Pacific region is underscored by its geo-economic realities. These include the fact that by 2040, the 40-odd countries in the region will comprise 65 percent of the world's population and 50 percent of its GDP, including five of the world's largest economies, China, India, Japan, South Korea and Australia. These five countries are expected to have a GDP of USD 29.3 trillion, as compared to USD 17.2 trillion for the 27 countries comprising the EU. The Indo-Pacific is also the world's fastest-growing region, with USD 47.19 trillion in economic activity. By 2030 the region will be home to two-thirds of the global middle class with substantial spending and investing power. All these factors will ensure that the Indo-Pacific remains the centre of global dynamism for the foreseeable future.[29] This, in turn, will ensure that the region will be a critical economic opportunity for developed nations in terms of investment, manufacturing and trade.

The IOR, part of the Indo-Pacific, directly impacts India's maritime security. The IOR's strategic importance stems from the fact, that apart from its indigenous mineral and non-mineral wealth, it is a critical throughway for transportation of crude, LPG, various commodities and finished goods between the manufacturing hubs in East, Southeast and South Asia, and their markets in the west coast of the Americas, Europe, Asia, Africa and the Middle-East. As per the United Nations Conference on Trade and Development figures, around 80 percent of global trade by volume and 70 percent by value, worth an estimated USD 28.5 trillion, was carried by sea in 2021,[30] reflecting the dependence of nations on the seas. Of this, over 80 percent of the world's maritime oil trade and over 60 percent of all global trade transits through the waters of the Indian Ocean; in 2020, over 1,45,000 ships operated in, or through the Indian Ocean, transporting oil and other raw materials, consumer goods, food and electronic products. The geography of the Indian Ocean dictates that access to the ocean is possible only through a number of choke points, principal among them being the Cape of Good Hope, the Suez Canal, and the straits of Bab-el-Mandeb, Hormuz, Malacca and Sunda. It is not inconceivable for malign states and non-state actors to block or disrupt these choke points, thereby adversely impacting energy security and economic well-being across the globe. India's strategic geographic location, astride the major sea-lanes of the world, points to the crucial relevance of its role in ensuring security and stability, and thereby the free flow of oil and commerce in the IOR.

The replacement of the Asia-Pacific concept with the Indo-Pacific concept over the past decade is a return to Spykman's Theory. India being the dominant resident Indian Ocean power is one of the two 'Book-ends' of the region, the other being the US. The west's strategy to contain China cannot be achieved without India's support. Concurrently, India too needs external support to balance its adverse power differential with a hostile and aggressive China which claims over 90,000 sq. km of Indian territory (besides being in illegal occupation of another 38,000 sq. km of its territory in Ladakh) and has actively connived with Pakistan over the past 70 years to tie India down. This congruence of interests between India and the West (including Japan and other democratic powers across the region) vis-à-vis China also implies support for building up India as a major power, much as was done to China in the 1980s to counter the Soviet Union, and gives India a free hand in the IOR, provided it builds up its maritime power.

Strategic Environment in the Indo-Pacific

A scan of the Indo-Pacific shows, that the region contains a widely varied mix of developed, developing and a few failed states with an equally varied systems of governance, from vibrant democracies to military dictatorships and authoritarian regimes. The vastness of the region and lack of homogeneity has also led to the absence of an over-arching security structure, with different security groupings existing in different sub-regions of the Indo-Pacific. Having been dominated by colonial powers from the 16th century to the mid-20th century, the region also has a number of unresolved land and maritime boundary disputes, most of which are a legacy of its colonial past. Not surprisingly, most of the major conflicts since the end of the Cold War have also taken place in the Indo-Pacific. As a consequence, the Indo-Pacific remains the centre of global maritime military deployments and contestation, dominated until the first decade of the 21st century, by the US Navy. However, as brought out earlier, this domination is being increasingly challenged by China.

Apart from traditional maritime military threats, the Indo-Pacific is also afflicted with a number of non-traditional maritime threats. These include low intensity maritime conflicts waged by state and non-state entities, conjoined with other global menaces such as terrorism, piracy, drug trafficking, gun-running and people trafficking. The adverse impact of climate change, manifesting in extreme weather-related disasters and sea-level rise, also presents security challenges to the region. Unsustainable fishing practices and massive dumping of plastics and other pollutants in the oceans have adversely impacted marine life in the oceans and the Indo-Pacific region is particularly affected by this issue. In 2017 it was reported that of 441 fish stocks, 47 percent were fully exploited, 18 percent were over-exploited, 9 percent were depleted and only 1 percent was recovering.[31] Given the vastness of the Indo-Pacific, concerted collective action is required to combat non-traditional threats to maritime security in the region.

While every nation is entitled to maintain forces for its defence, the current international unease stems from the unprecedented build-up of the PLA Navy (PLAN) and the opacity of China's intentions. The PLAN's extensive deployment in the IOR and beyond, under the guise of anti-piracy patrols; as also the aggression displayed by China in the South China Sea to usurp islets and reefs, and subsequently restrict freedom of movement in its waters, displays a contempt for a rule-based international order and China's belief that 'Might is Right'. Today, the PLAN outmatches every regional navy in Asia, and in the past few years, it has surpassed the US Navy in total numbers of major combatants. Indeed, by the end of 2023, the PLAN had 328 major surface combatants (not including 60 missile-armed patrol vessels/smaller combatants), as compared to the US Navy's 289 battle-force ships; and is predicted to grow to 400 major combatants by 2025 and 425 by 2030. The US itself acknowledges that the PLAN poses a major challenge to their ability to maintain wartime sea control in ocean areas of the western Pacific, the first such challenge posed to the US Navy since the end of the Cold War.

The apprehension that China's maritime strategy aims to not only build up its military power, but also to use that power to secure resources, trade routes, export markets and overseas bases for the eventual realisation of the 'Chinese Dream', is exemplified by China's BRI. The maritime section of the BRI initiative, the 'Maritime Silk Route' (MSR), is a continuation of the so-called 'String of Pearls' strategy of developing maritime infrastructure in the IOR, commenced by China in the mid-1990s. This has its origins in China's anxiety over its 'Malacca Dilemma'. Being overly dependent on energy supplies and having access to export markets through the choke-points of the Indian Ocean, China commenced building maritime infrastructure and overland oil pipelines along its major sea lines of communication in the IOR at the turn of the 21st century. This was transformed into a mammoth blueprint for the construction of infrastructure, harbours, roads, power plants, etc., the final design of which was released in the form of the BRI on 28 Mar 2015.

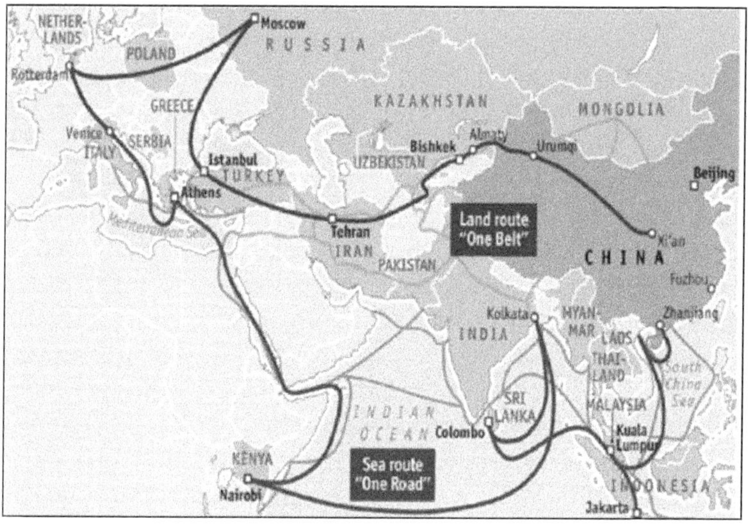

Figure 3 - The Belt and Road Initiative as viewed from China[32]

With proposed investments of almost USD 1 trillion, the use of the BRI by China to employ its over-capacity in infrastructure creation and foreign exchange reserves, support its exports and project its influence in the Indo-Pacific region, matches perfectly with its mercantilist approach of 'Trade follows flag'. This method of 'Economic Diplomacy' is also in line with western colonial mercantilist policy in the 18th and 19th centuries, where economics and politics were inextricably inter-twined.

Hence, despite its branding as an economic and development initiative, the BRI is in fact the embodiment of a whole-of-government approach to develop the close coordination between military struggle and diplomatic, economic, cultural and legal endeavours that Xi Jinping has called for, to foster a strategic environment conducive to China's rise. Driven by steady economic growth, which even the COVID-19 pandemic has not been able to dampen significantly, the current trend is clearly towards an increasingly Chinese-dominated political, economic, technological, and strategic ecosystem in the Indo-Pacific. The challenge posed by the BRI lies not just in enhanced PLA capabilities, but in Beijing's greater ability to project its influence, based on a unilateral assertion of 'Core interests'. The exercise of this power challenges the current rule-based international order.

While China has strenuously insisted that the BRI is solely about economic cooperation and does not have any military component, it had said much the same about the reclaimed islands in the South China Sea, which have now been militarised. Similarly, despite promising for several decades that it would never set-up overseas military bases, China's first such base was established in Djibouti in 2017. Thus, there is deep global suspicion that the BRI is a Trojan horse for China's strategic military ambitions, which will not only support its economic growth, but also provide it leverage to obtain military bases, particularly from weak and indebted countries along the BRI. This is bolstered by the fact that several BRI port projects, such as Gwadar and Hambantota, located in strategic proximity to vital sea lanes and maritime chokepoints in the Indo-Pacific, do not appear to be driven by commercial logic. China's 2019 Defence White Paper has also included 'Protection of China's overseas interests' as a new mission for the PLA. This has been justified by the fact that China's overseas investments and properties now roughly amount to USD 7 trillion, with over 5.5 million Chinese citizens living overseas, with both figures set to grow exponentially with the BRI. While the progress of the BRI has languished after the COVID-19 pandemic and the Ukraine War, with several participant countries falling into a debt trap, and China's economic progress itself seems to have slowed substantially, the gains made thus far in the maritime sphere are still adequate to progress China's eventual dream of becoming a 'Great Power'.

The recent invasion of Ukraine by Russia, and the developing China-Russia axis after their joint statement in Feb 2022, has introduced a new equation into the Indo-Pacific by re-focusing attention from the Asia-Pacific and Euro-Atlantic. The Ukraine war is a win-win situation for China, and it is evident that China seeks a weakened Russia as a junior partner and a source for cheap raw materials in its quest to dominate the world. Besides, the conflict would distract the current US focus from the Indo-Pacific, as was the case during the Cold War, thereby giving China a freer rein in the region. Whatever be the outcome, the importance of the Indo-Pacific region is unlikely to diminish in the decades ahead.

India's Indo-Pacific Moment

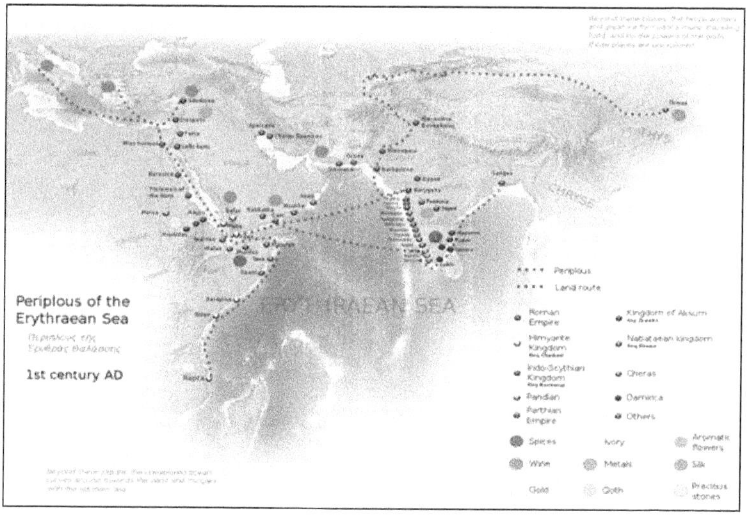

Figure 4 - Periplous of the Erythraean Sea[33]

India has had a long maritime history dating back to antiquity, with the first references to maritime activities being contained in the *Rig Veda*. Excavations at Lothal in Gujarat have revealed the remains of a dockyard dating back to 2500 to 1700 BCE, the oldest such structure found anywhere in the world. Substantial literary and archaeological evidence of our ancient and medieval maritime prowess is available, which indicates that India had flourishing trade relations with ancient Rome, the Egyptian and Mesopotamian civilisations through the Red Sea and the Persian Gulf dating back to 3000 BCE, thousands of years before European maritime powers discovered the sea route to India. The '*Periplous of the Erythraean Sea*' (Figure 4) is one such record that shows the trading routes that existed between India and Rome, Egypt and ancient Middle Eastern civilisations around the 1st century CE.

Several ancient Indian kingdoms and empires, such as the *Kalinga* (1700 to 3 BCE), the *Maurya* (321 to 185 BCE), the *Gupta* (300 to 543 CE), *Satavahana* (200 BCE to 250 CE), *Pallava* (275 to 897 CE), *Chola* (200 to 1279 CE), Pandya (3 BCE to 14th century CE), *Chera* (300 BCE to 300 CE), *Chera Perumal* (9 to 12 CE) and *Vijayanagara* (1336 to 1646 CE) maintained substantial maritime power, which spread Indian thought and trade as far afield as Japan and as far west as Europe. Probably the best known use of India's maritime tradition was to spread Buddhism to Southeast Asia, East Asia and Sri Lanka. This was exemplified by the voyage to Sri Lanka in 288 BCE by Emperor Ashoka's eldest daughter, Princess Sangamitra (282 to 203 BCE), carrying a cutting of the Bodhi tree and Lord Buddha's tooth relic. Today known as the *Jaya Shri Maha Bodhi*, the tree still stands at Anuradhapura and is revered as the oldest living human planted tree in the world, while the 'Temple of the Tooth' at Kandy is Sri Lanka's most revered Buddhist temple.

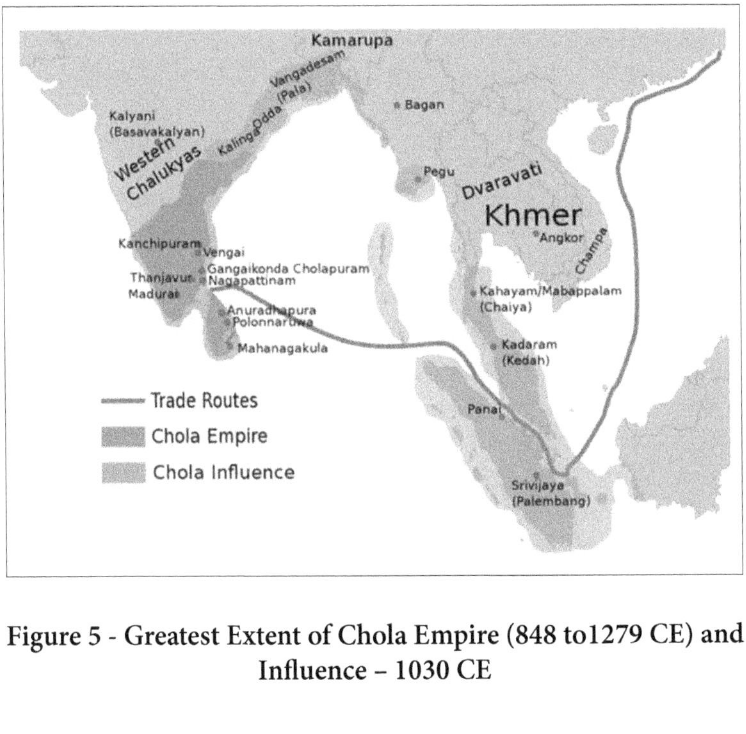

Figure 5 - Greatest Extent of Chola Empire (848 to1279 CE) and Influence – 1030 CE

The decline of India's maritime tradition started with the advent of the Mongols in North India, after the fall of the Gupta Empire in the 5th century. The arrival of the Mughals in the 14th century, who were to be the pre-dominant power in India for the next four centuries, and were more conversant with land than the oceans, sealed the fate of maritime India. As a result, when the Portuguese appeared off Calicut in 1498, guided by a Gujarati navigator, the Indian Ocean was bereft of any indigenous naval power. Despite the gallant efforts of a few, most notably the Marathas and the Zamorins of Calicut, colonial maritime powers, starting with the Portuguese, then the Dutch and French, and finally the British, held sway over the waters of the Indian Ocean, till India's independence in 1947. In his book, 'India and the Indian Ocean', KM Panikkar wrote that "Despite countless invasions from India's northwest border over centuries, India never lost her independence till she lost command of the sea in the first decade of the 16th Century". The result of the maritime superiority of European maritime powers was the gradual colonisation of not just the Indian sub-continent, but also most of Africa, Southeast Asia and Australia. The economic and cultural decline of the colonised countries was also a direct consequence of their neglect of the seas.

While re-building of the Indian Navy (*IN*) started soon after independence, it was only after the Cold War ended in 1990 that India saw a more coordinated use of its Navy in concert with some foreign policy objectives, the initiation of the Malabar Exercises with the US Navy and the MILAN Exercises with Bay of Bengal rim navies were not merely military interactions but also contained powerful political messages. The fact that US elevated Indo-US relations to the strategic plane and India became a sectoral dialogue partner of ASEAN in 1992, a full dialogue partner in 1995 (elevated to ASEAN+1 in 2003), as also a member of the ASEAN Regional Forum in 1996, could be attributed to the successful integration of India's diplomatic, economic and military (mainly maritime) strategies in the region. The economic diplomacy initiated with the 'Look East' policy specifically re-invigorated India's military ties with key Southeast Asian countries such as Indonesia, Vietnam and Singapore. Notably, India's economic liberalisation in 1991 also coincided with the re-commencement of the *IN's* role in building security partnerships with key allies in the Indo-Pacific, an implicit recognition of the close connection between economic prosperity and maritime security. It is not surprising that economic relations between India and ASEAN also blossomed in 1992. Since, the India-ASEAN Free Trade Agreement was signed in 2009, bilateral trade has increased from USD 420 million in 1995 to USD 131.5 billion in 2022 ,[34] amply demonstrating the synergy between trade and maritime engagement. This has been replicated since with a host of other countries in the Indo-Pacific and beyond.

The unshackling of India's economy has ensured India's steady economic progress over the past three decades. As per 2023 International Monetary Fund (IMF) data, with a nominal GDP of USD 3.7 trillion, India ranks fifth behind the US (USD 26.8 trillion), China (USD 19.3 trillion), Japan (USD 4.4 trillion) and Germany (USD 4.2 trillion). PM Modi had stated in Jul 2023 that India would become the world's third largest economy by 2029, after the US and China.[35] Long range predictions anticipate that India will overtake the US as the second largest economy (in purchasing power parity terms) by 2047, with a 20 percent share of global GDP. Recently, PM Modi has also set a goal of India becoming a developed nation by 2047, the centenary of our independence.[36] A necessary characteristic of a developed country is high per capita income, USD 21,664 as per the IMF. A research article by the Reserve Bank of India states that India's economy will have to grow at a sustained rate of 7.6 percent or more per annum over the next 25 years to achieve this feat by 2047. However, with a current per capita income of USD 2,601, we still rank 139th out of 183 countries. Indeed, India has more poor people than any other country in the world. It is also important to note that since 1991 India's economy has grown over 7.6 percent only seven times and has not been able to sustain this pace for more than two consecutive years. While India's trend growth rate has been increasing, and many economists estimate our potential growth rate to be 7 percent, maintaining a consistent growth rate above 7.5 percent is a tall order.[37]

That of course does not mean that our endeavour of becoming a developed economy by 2047 is unachievable, only that, it requires all sectors of India's economy to fire consistently on all cylinders to achieve the required growth rate. For example, India needs to rebalance its economic structure by strengthening its industrial sector so that its share in GDP rises from the current level of 25.6 percent to around 35 percent by 2047 .[38] While India needs to do several things to achieve this growth, such as reducing inequality, focusing on health and education to improve innovation and productivity, etc., this essay argues that the maritime sector is a key enabler to achieve this target, which is today performing sub-optimally, as existing facts demonstrate.

India's Marine Economy

The American economist Gerald J. Mangon (1982) first introduced the concept of the 'Marine Economy' defining it as 'An economic activity that takes marine resources as an input'. The Organisation for Economic Co-operation and Development defines the 'Ocean Economy' as 'The sum of the economic activities of ocean-based industries, together with assets, goods and services provided by marine ecosystems'.[39] India's share of global trade is relatively small, accounting for less than 2.5 percent of merchandise trade and less than 4 percent of services trade.[40] While 95 percent of India's trade by volume and 68 percent by value moves through ocean routes, the share of Indian ships in the carriage of India's EXIM trade has declined from 40.7 percent in 1987 to 1988 to about 7.8 percent in 2018 to 2019. India's merchant shipping fleet comprised 1491 vessels in 2021 (1027 coastal and 464 overseas)[41] and was ranked 19th in the world in terms of capacity of dead weight tonnage (1.3 percent of total global tonnage).[42] The main reason for this decline is that the operating costs of Indian ships are 20 percent more than foreign ships, on account of higher interest on loans for shipping companies and higher taxation rates in India.

The decline of India's national shipping fleet reduces India's economic, commercial and strategic advantages. A strong and diverse Indian fleet will save massive amounts of foreign exchange, India paid foreign shipping companies of around USD 637 billion in the period 2008 to 2021.[43] It will also reduce over-dependence on foreign carriers for the transportation of Indian cargo, an aspect that would be critical during hostilities or crises. China dominates world shipping today and a substantial part of global (and Indian) trade is carried in Chinese flagged/owned vessels, which could face disruption in the case of a conflict, a critical supply chain for which we need to build resilience. A strong Indian shipping fleet would also increase training opportunities and employment of seafarers, besides financial benefits to the exchequer due to the generation of greater revenue.

As far as the shipbuilding and ship repair sectors are concerned, the situation is similar. India has 28 shipyards, six under the Central Public Sector, two under State Governments and 20 under the Private Sector. India is ranked 15th in global shipbuilding with only 0.12 percent of global ships having been built in India in 2021. In terms of ports, India has 12 major and about 200 non-major ports which handled a total cargo of 1320 million tons in 2019 to 2020. However, only two ports, Mundra (26) and Nhava Sheva (28), figure among the 50 busiest ports in the world. The global ship repair and maintenance market is expected to reach a value of USD 40 billion by 2028. India's share in this business is less than 1 percent though there is substantial scope for it to expand substantially due to benefits of a cheap and skilled workforce.[44] While India is the third largest fish producing country in the world, most of its fishing fleet comprises coastal and artisanal fishing. In terms of other maritime power metrics, such as ocean scientific research, underwater exploration/mining, etc., India lags behind many countries.

In comparison, China is the leading manufacturer of ships and shipping equipment in the world, producing 96 percent of the shipping containers, 80 percent of ship-to-shore cranes and received 48 percent of the world's shipbuilding orders in 2020.[45] Apart from having seven of the ten busiest ports in the world, China owns over 100 ports in 63 countries, operated by the state-owned port operators, China Ocean Shipping Company, China Merchants Group, and CK Hutchison Holdings. These include ports in Sri Lanka (Hambantota), Pakistan (Gwadar), France (Le Havre and Dunkirk), Djibouti (Port Djibouti), Belgium (Antwerp and Bruges), Italy (Vado), Spain (Noatum), Turkey (Kumport),

Greece (Piraeus), Israel (Haifa), Cuba (Santiago de Cuba), Brazil (TCP Participaccoes SA), and Peru (Port of Chancay). Negotiations are undergoing for taking over ports in El Salvador, Bahamas, Trinidad and Tobago, Panama, Argentina, Chile and Uruguay. China also partially owns port terminals in the US in Houston, Florida, Seattle and Los Angeles. China's global maritime dominance is evident from the comparison of the maritime profiles of India, China and the US at Table 1.

Metrics	US	China	India
GDP [USD mn]	23,111,315	17,298,593	3,171,347
Merchandise Trade [EXIM in USD mn]	4,689,615	60,052,469	9,68,334
Transport Services Trade [EXIM in USD mn]	1,345,298	8,33,510	1,95,956
Ship-building [Ships > 100 Gross tonnage (GT), in thousands of GT]	32,343	26,863,204	72,137
Fleet – National Flag [numbers of ships > 100 GT/in thousands of Deadweight Tonnage (DWT)]	3,637 12,537	6,937 108,481	1,811 17,123
Fleet – Ownership [Ships > 1000 GT, in thousands of DWT]	54,907	246,738	26,417
Number of Seafarers	59,586	134,294	113,474
Container Throughput [Twenty-Foot Equivalent Unit]	56,963,689	245,103,781	16,285,806
Ship Recycling [Ships > 100 GT, in thousands of GT]	76,566	140,112	2,699,541

Table 1 - Maritime Profile Comparison of the US, China and India – 20 Oct 2022[46]

China actively monitors its marine economy, which is divided into three sectors – primary, secondary and tertiary. It has been estimated, based on figures published by China's State Oceanic Administration that China's maritime economy contributed to about 10 percent of China's GDP in the period 2000 to 2019[47] (Table 2). China's marine economy was expected to reach a value of 10 trillion Yuan in 2022.[48]

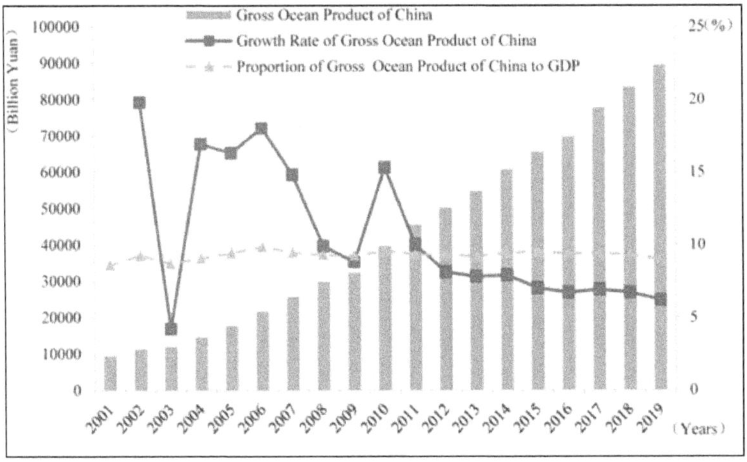

Figure 6 - China Ocean Statistics Yearbook (2002 to 2017): Marine Economic Statistics Bulletin (2017 to 2019)

As far as India is concerned, according to the Ministry of Shipping report of 2020, the marine sector of India (ports and shipping, coastal shipping, inland waterways, shipbuilding and repair, and maritime services) contributes around 5 percent of India's GDP.[49] Of this, the port and shipping sector comprises 1.4 percent, coastal shipping and inland waterways around 0.3 percent and 0.1 percent, respectively, and the shipbuilding and repair sector 0.4 percent, while marine services account for the largest chunk i.e., 2.1 percent. India's marine sector is also a significant employer, providing direct and indirect employment to over 14 mn people. There is, therefore, the substantial scope for India's marine economy to grow, and if it can double its contribution to the country's GDP, it would provide our economy an additional boost for sustained growth of 7.5 percent and above. Recognising the importance of the maritime sector, the Government of India has taken several steps over the past two decades to provide it with impetus, with the major initiatives as follows:

- **National Maritime Development Programme (NMDP)**. The NMDP was launched in 2005 to increase the capacity and efficiency of ports, enhance maritime connectivity, promote coastal shipping, and develop shipbuilding and repair facilities. Under this scheme, the government has invested in development of new ports, modernisation of existing ports and establishment of maritime training institutes.

- **Sagarmala Programme**. The Sagarmala programme was pre-dated by the Maritime Agenda 2010 to 2020. Launched in 2015, it is aimed at port-led development and harnessing the potential of India's coastline and maritime sector. Initiatives such as Sagarmala are expected to provide additional employment to around 10 million people. As of Dec 2021, the programme had identified 802 projects worth 5.54 lakh crore for implementation till 2035 in multiple sectors including port modernisation, connectivity, coastal community development, coastal tourism, etc., that aim to generate employment, increase industrial output and reduce logistics costs.[50]

- **Maritime India Vision 2030**. In 2016, the Government of India launched the Maritime India Vision 2030, which outlines the vision and strategy for the development of India's maritime sector over the next decade.[51] This vision aims to double the port capacity to 2600 million tons, establish three new major ports, increase the share of India's global shipbuilding, repair and recycling, enhance maritime connectivity, and promote coastal tourism. The programme also envisages the establishment of maritime clusters and the development of maritime infrastructure. Coastal shipping and inland waterways have also been identified for development.

➢ **Global India Maritime Summits**. India held the third edition of the Global India Maritime Summit in Oct 2023, which was aimed to attract global and domestic investment in the maritime sector. During his address at the summit, PM Modi stated that India was aspiring to be among the five top ship-building countries by 2047 and was also investing in green technologies in shipping and other maritime sectors as part of its drive to develop India's blue economy. He also released the '*Amrit Kaal* Vision 2047', a blueprint for India's maritime blue economy. The summit is reported to have helped India secure investments of INR 10 lakh crore in the maritime sector.[52]

➢ **Green Port Initiative**. This was launched in 2016 to promote the adoption of green technologies and practices in Indian ports to reduce environmental pollution, improve energy efficiency and gain carbon credits. The initiative focuses on enhancing power from renewable energy sources, energy efficient lighting, waste management and reduction of emissions from port-related activities.

➢ **Ease of Doing Business Reforms**. While the 'Ease of doing business reforms' are meant to apply to all sectors, for the marine sector, they specifically include: single-window clearances for port-related activities, simplification of customs procedures, and reduction in time periods for cargo clearance. The reforms aim to attract more investment into India's marine sector and encourage entrepreneurship.

➢ **'Make in India' Programme**. Defence shipbuilding has always been a national leader in defence indigenisation under the active patronage of the *IN* since the early 1960s. Since the launch of the 'Make in India' programme in 2014, 80 percent of the Acceptance of Necessity on cost basis have been awarded to Indian vendors, mainly Defence Public Sector Undertakings (DPSUs). Almost 90 percent of ship repair by value of IN ships is also undertaken in Indian shipyards. With four DPSU shipbuilders and two other major shipyards, Cochin Shipyard Ltd., which builds and refits aircraft carriers, and Larsen and Toubro, which is involved in both submarine and defence shipbuilding, India has excellent potential to become a regional hub of defence shipbuilding and repair. However, the story of civil shipbuilding is not as rosy as indicated in Table 1 above. The reason for this has been unfriendly government policies over the past seven decades, as also strong competition from Japan, China and South Korea, who are able to build ships faster and at much lower prices than India. One reason for China's rise as the world's second largest shipbuilder has been the massive subsidies provided for the shipping industry by the Chinese government amounting to USD 132 billion between 2010 and 2018.[53]

While the programmes initiated by the government have had a positive impact, they have not been able to galvanise the entire sector to the extent desired. Much more needs to be done to enable India's marine sector to enhance its contribution to India's GDP.

India's Maritime Security Interests and Opportunities

India has substantial maritime interests, which it needs to protect. 87.3 percent of crude oil requirements and over 50 percent of its natural gas requirements were imported in the financial year 2022 to 2023, all over the sea (over 60 percent from the Persian Gulf). Of the 12.7 percent indigenous production of crude oil, 67 percent is from India's Exclusive Economic Zone (EEZ). India's seaborne trade in 2021 to 2022 was valued at around USD 1035 billion (USD 422 billion in exports and USD 613 billion in imports)[54]and this figure is set to grow considerably. India's EEZ is almost equal to its land mass with great potential for sustainable exploitation of its blue economy. A large percentage of India's major energy infrastructure is located on its coast. India is also fortunate to have island territories off both coasts, which not only extend its EEZ substantially, but are also strategic springboards into the Indian Ocean.

At the same time, India faces formidable conventional and non-conventional maritime threats in the IOR. It needs to combat/ deter conventional maritime threats from China and Pakistan in the IOR; and cater to the maritime implications of the several military conflict flashpoints with global ramifications in the Indo-Pacific such as Taiwan, North Korea, South China Sea, Iran and Yemen. Countering piracy, armed robbery, terrorism, drug trafficking, human smuggling, gun running, Illegal, Unreported and Unregulated (IUU) fishing, etc., also remain perennial tasks, requiring the commitment of dedicated force levels. New maritime challenges include the need to meet the threats arising from climate change as a result of global warming: natural disasters, ocean degradation and loss of biodiversity, displacement of coastal populations due to rises in sea levels, and the resulting adverse impact on internal and regional security.

The dependence of Indo-Pacific littorals on the oceans for their prosperity and well-being requires a stable, secure and law-abiding littoral, which can only be guaranteed by maritime forces working in concert. Many Indo-Pacific littorals being small island states or developing countries require both capability and capacity inputs to ensure their maritime security and realise the potential of their blue economies. As is evident, there are a number of other matters, such as search and rescue, pollution control, marine scientific research, hydrography, etc., where most Indo-Pacific littorals do not have the necessary expertise, resources or capacity. Maritime power is expensive and not within the reach of everyone, and yet national sovereignty is sacrosanct. It is India's experience that smaller nations in the IOR not only look up to India for help and support, but also expect the *IN* to safeguard their maritime interests in many ways. India's democratic credentials, its commitment to international agreements and laws, its close diplomatic relations with almost all countries in the region, and its ancient philosophy of *Vasudhaiva Kutumbakam* makes it a trusted and reliable ally. In addition, the apolitical and professional nature of the *IN* makes it an ideal partner for the maritime forces of other countries.

Mahan had listed six essential attributes for a country to become a maritime power in his seminal work 'The Influence of Sea Power on History', which included: geographical position; physical conformation; extent of territory; size of population;

character of the people; and character of the government. India has the first four attributes in ample measure but is deficient in the last two. However, the two deficient attributes are amenable to change, as China has demonstrated successfully over the past four decades. Indeed, India has taken a number of concrete steps to focus national attention on its maritime security. India's maritime policy is encapsulated by the acronym SAGAR (Security and Growth for All in the Region), articulated by Prime Minister Modi in 2015. Prime Minister Modi announced the Indo-Pacific Oceans' Initiative at the 14th East Asia Summit in 2019 and chaired the first high-level open debate on 'Enhancing Maritime Security – A Case for International Cooperation' at the United Nation Security Council in Aug 2021.

In absence of any pan Indo-Pacific security arrangement, besides intensifying bilateral maritime security engagements with individual countries of the Indo-Pacific, India is also engaged in maritime security constructs at the trilateral and plutilateral levels. QUAD is the most prominent plurilateral platform that addresses contemporary challenges and opportunities in the Indo-Pacific. The energies of the QUAD are directed at a broad range of activities ranging from maritime safety and security, humanitarian assistance and disaster recovery, cyber security, critical and emerging technologies, connectivity, education, health and space cooperation. The *IN* engages with other QUAD navies in advanced naval exercises to build interoperability and strengthen maritime security. India is also an integral part of the QUAD's Indo-Pacific Maritime Domain Awareness Initiative, which focuses on maritime safety, IUU fishing and mitigating the consequences of natural disasters.

These initiatives, while laudable, need to be followed up with a concrete action plan to ensure that India grows its Comprehensive Maritime Power (CMP) in a time-bound manner and assumes responsibility as the pre-eminent maritime power in the IOR.

Developing India's Comprehensive Maritime Power

The adoption of the Indo-Pacific construct by a majority of the global community points not only to the importance of the region to the globe as a whole, but also to the importance of India to the region. Global power shifts are rare occurrences and it should not be taken for granted that the Indo-Pacific will retain its current pre-eminence forever. As aptly stated in Shakespeare's 'Julius Caesar', "There is a tide in the affairs of men; which, taken at the flood, leads on to fortune". This phrase is particularly relevant to India, as far the development of its CMP is concerned, at the current juncture of 'the rising tide' of India's fortunes.

CMP can best be defined as 'The sum total of the maritime power of a country, encompassing its political, economic, commercial, military, constabulary, technological, scientific, legal and soft power dimensions'.[55] As evident from the definition, CMP can be divided broadly between 'Maritime Hard Power', which includes the dimensions of political, economic, commercial, military, constabulary, technological, scientific and legal power; and 'Maritime Soft Power', which encompasses the benign dimensions of search and rescue, hydrography, climate change mitigation activities, humanitarian assistance and disaster relief, medical assistance and research, tourism and maritime sports, maritime history and archaeology, salvage, international maritime scientific and academic research, international conservation efforts, etc.

Specific attention needs to be directed towards the development of India's marine economy, as it is foundational to the development of India's CMP. In this, efforts to revive our shipbuilding sector and our national shipping fleet, merit special attention. Both of these sectors will require substantial and continued government support and subsidies, as China's example shows. These are difficult obstacles to overcome, as the World Trade Organisation and other international and national agreements and guidelines would need to be dealt with. However, without adequate national capability in both these sectors, India will remain a second-rate maritime power. India's positive experience in defence shipbuilding, where we have successfully built an aircraft carrier and strategic and conventional submarines clearly indicates that we have the requisite technical and human expertise to expand indigenous shipbuilding in the non-military sector as well. The long term economic and strategic benefits of reviving these sectors are worth the investment.

As brought out before, the aim should be to double the contribution of the marine sector to India's GDP from the current 5 percent to at least 9 to 10 percent. Focusing on the economic contribution of the marine sector is of fundamental importance, for economic growth alone will provide funds for military modernisation (among other national needs). As an example, despite a seven-fold increase in China's military spending over the past two decades, China's economic growth has ensured that its defence spending as a percentage of overall government expenditure has dropped significantly over the years.

It is also critical to prevent a maritime military imbalance with other major powers, especially China. While the *IN* today is among the top ten navies of the world, there is a large gap between the first three navies (US, China and Russia) and the others. Navies, unlike armies and air forces, are built over long periods of time. Therefore, sequential ship and submarine building programmes, with sustained capital funding are essential to maintain adequate and technologically relevant maritime forces. Gaps in funding and delays in sanctioning projects and in shipbuilding can cause serious capability voids, which once created require decades of efforts to revive. It is, therefore, essential that the integrated capability development plan of the armed forces pays serious attention to reviving the *IN's* force levels, apart from investing in offset technologies and strategies, to redress the current imbalance with our principal adversary China.

Since a developing country such as India, will necessarily have competing requirements between guns and butter, there is an urgent need to promulgate an Indian model of China's Military-Civil Fusion (MCF) to synergise the defence and civilian sectors. By pooling infrastructure, human resources, industry, educational and research institutions, logistics support, etc., China has enabled economy of effort, the development of dual-use technologies, and in general, better harnessed national resources towards a common goal. There are many aspects of MCF worthy of emulation. For example, the Sagarmala plan should be closely linked with the development plan for maritime military infrastructure. Indian-flagged merchant ships could be outfitted for military use in case of hostilities and India's vast fishing fleet could be adequately equipped and utilised as eyes and ears at sea to bolster our surveillance capability, as done by China.

For both economy of effort and better operational synergy, India needs to implement structures to cater for the recognised importance of jointness and integration in modern warfare. China had clearly identified the importance of jointness and integration in modern battlefields after the first Gulf War, and since the 1990s, it has progressed steadily on this path. The sweeping military reforms announced in 2015, whereby theatre and functional commands were created, have synergised the PLA's military power, and focussed their attention on new fields of warfare, such as space, cyber and electromagnetic, besides giving primacy to maritime power. Such reforms in India, while planned, have been moving at a glacial pace and need to be expedited.

As is evident from the aforesaid, since the maritime arena encompasses a range of departments of the Government of India, India needs to take a comprehensive national approach to the development of its CMP as follows:

- All aspects of non-military maritime power, such as maritime infrastructure, ship-building and ship repair, technology, human resources, financial regulations, oceanographic research, fisheries, maritime archaeology, etc., need to be part of a comprehensive maritime strategy, preferably under the directions of the NITI Aayog.

- The development and coordination of all national and state maritime security agencies, such as the *IN*, Coast Guard, maritime police, etc. needs to be synergised under a comprehensive umbrella maritime security strategy, preferably under the Ministry of Defence.

- There is also an urgent need to promulgate an Indian model of China's MCF to synergise the maritime security and civilian sectors, ideally under the National Security Advisor.

➢ The appointment of the National Maritime Security Coordinator is a good example of a coordinating office in the field of national maritime security, which needs to be emulated for the overall maritime sector also, preferably at the ministerial level, directly under the PM's Office.

Conclusion

With strong economic growth, favourable demography, a democratic polity, soft power born out of civilisational strength, and a conducive international environment, India has a historic opportunity to regain its ancient 'Great Power' status. The oceans and maritime power will play a major role in achieving this goal. With two nuclear-armed adversaries' intent on blocking our continental overtures, our favourable maritime geography provides us with an oceanic highway to economic growth and global leadership. The Indo-Pacific construct benefits India and places us as a key player in the geo-politics of the entire region.

While India is already the natural maritime leader in the IOR and is looked upon as the preferred security partner by most IOR littorals, the mantle of regional or global leadership will not automatically gravitate to India. It needs to be earned by strengthening our comprehensive maritime power through an all-encompassing maritime strategy. China's explosive maritime growth and its growing presence in the IOR add urgency to India's need to focus on its maritime growth. Indeed, India's aspirations of attaining developed nation status by 2049, and becoming a 'Great Power' in the future, will also require strengthening all dimensions of maritime power, especially our marine economy. For history has proved that no country has attained 'Great Power' status without commensurate maritime power.

End Notes

1 Geoffrey Till and Patrick C Bratton (Eds), "Sea Power and the Rise and Fall of The Empires" in "Sea Power and the Asia-Pacific: The Triumph of Neptune?" Routledge, London and New York, 2012, 6

2 Alfred Thayer Mahan, "The Influence of Sea Power upon History – 1660-1783", Dover Publications Inc., New York, 1987, Preface, iv-v

3 Edward Ingram, "The British Empire as a World Power: Ten Studies", Frank Cass, London, 2000, pp.126-7

4 Jeff Desjardins, "Over 2,000 years of economic history, in one chart", Economic Progress, 15 September 2017, https://www.weforum.org/agenda/2017/09/over-2000-years-of-economic-history-in-one-chart

5 Mackinder, HJ "The Geographical Pivot of History", Democratic Ideals and Reality, Norton and Company, New York, 1962, 261

6 Nicholas John Spykman, "The Geography of the Peace", Harcourt, Brace and Company, New York, 1944, 52

7 Martin D. Mitchell, "Using the principles of Halford J. Mackinder and Nicholas John Spykman to re-evaluate a twenty-first-century geopolitical framework for the United States", Comparative Strategy, September 2020, 39:5, 407-424, https://doi.org/10.1080/01495933.2020.1803709

8 "Limits of Oceans and Seas, 3rd Edition", International Hydrographic Organisation, 1953, https://epic.awi.de/id/eprint/29772/1/IHO1953a.pdf, 22, 34-35

9 El Nino/ La Nina Southern Oscillation (ENSO), World Meteorological Organisation, https://public.wmo.int/en/our-mandate/el-ni%3C%B1ola-ni%C%B1a-update

10 Hansong Li, "The "Indo-Pacific": Intellectual Origins and International Visions in Global Contexts", Modern Intellectual History, Cambridge University Press, 04 June 2021, https://www.cambridge.org/core/journals/ modern-intellectual-history/article/indopacific-intellectual-origins-and-international-visions-in-global-context/21B142B132F694349D46CAD22EA8C7CD

11 "Confluence of the Two Seas", Speech by HE Shinzo Abe, Prime Minister of Japan at the Parliament of the epublic of India, 22 August

2007, MOFA, Government of Japan, https://www.mofa.go.jp/region/asia-paci/pmv0708/speech-.html

12 Gurpreet S. Khurana, "Security of Sea Lines: Prospects for India-Japan Cooperation", Strategic Analysis, 31:1, https://idsa.in/strategic analysis/SecurityofSeaLinesProspectsforIndiaJapanCooperation_gskhurana_0107, 139-153

13 "National Security Strategy of the United States of America", December 2017, The White House, Washington DC, https://trumpwhitehouse.archives.gov/wp-content/uploads/2017/2017/12/NSS-Final-12-18-2017-0905.pdf, 45-47

14 "The Indo-Pacific Strategy of the United States", February 2022, The White House, Washington DC, https://www.whitehouse.gov/wp-content/Uploads/2022/02/U.S.-Indo-Pacific-Strategy.pdf, 4

15 "France's Indo-Pacific Strategy", Government of France, February 2022, https://www.diplomatie.gouv.fr/IMG/pdf/en_dcp_a4_indopacifique_022022_v1_4_web_cle878143.pdf

16 "Policy Guidelines for the Indo-Pacific Region: Germany – Europe – Asia: Shaping the 21 st Century Together", The Federal Government, September 2020, https://rangun.diplo.de/blob2380824/a27b62057f2d2675ce2bbfc5be01099a/policy-guidelines-summary-data.pdf

17 "Joint Communication to the European Parliament and the Council – The EU Strategy for Cooperation in the Indo-Pacific", European Union, Brussels, 16 September 2021, https://www.eeas.europa.eu/eeas/joint-communication-indo-pacific_en, 2

18 "PM's Keynote Address at Shangri La Dialogue", PMINDIA, 01 June 2018, https:/www.pmindia.gov.in/en/news_updates/pms-kenote-address-at-shangri-la-dialogue

19 "China's share of global gross domestic product (GDP) adjusted for purchasing-power-parity (PPP) from 1980 to 2022 with forecasts until 2028", Statista,12 April 2023, https://www.statista.com/statistics/270439/chinas-share-of-global-gross-domestic-product-gdp/

20 "China's National Defence in 2004", http://www.china.org.cn/e-white/20041227/, 9

21 Tom (Guorui) Sun and Alex Payette, "China's Two Ocean Strategy:

Controlling Waterways and the New Silk Road", Asia Focus # 31, May 2017, Institut de Realtions Internationales et Strategiques, https://www.iris-france.org/wp-content/uploads/2017/05/Asia-Focus-31.pdf

22 China Aerospace Studies Institute, "In their Own Words: Foreign Military Thought, The Science of Military Strategy (2013)", (English translation of the book written by the Academy of Military Sciences of the People's Liberation Army of China), February 2021, https://www.airuniversity.af.edu/Portals/10/CASI/documents/ Translations/2021-02-08%20 Chinese%20Military%20 Thoughts-%20In%20their %20own%20words%20Science %20 of%20Military%20 Strategy%202013.pdf?ver=TdMNn2O9Ktebbf6tMzgT6g%3d%3d

23 Ibid, The Science of Military Strategy, 105-6

24 Ibid, The Science of Military Strategy, 247

25 Ibid, "Joint Communication to the European Parliament and the Council – The EU Strategy for Cooperation in the Indo-Pacific", 6

26 Ibid, "The Indo-Pacific Strategy of the United States", 5

27 Ibid, The Science of Military Strategy (2013), 247

28 Andrew S. Erickson, "Power vs. Distance: China's Global Maritime Interests and Investments in the Far Seas", China's Expanding Strategic Ambitions, (Eds) Ashley Tellis, Alison Szalwinski and Michael Wills, The National Bureau of Asian Research, 2019, 253

29 "Canada's Indo-Pacific Strategy", 24 July 2023, https://www.international.gc.ca/transparency-transparence/indo-pacific-indo-pacifique/index.aspx?lang=eng

30 "Global trade hits record high of $28.5 trillion in 2021, but likely to be subdued in 2022", UNCTAD, 17 February 2022, https://unctad.org/new/global-trade-hits-record-high-285-trillion-2021-likely-to-be-subdued-2022

31 "Fisheries Management", IORA, 2017, https://www.iora.int/en/priorities-focus-area/fisheries-management

32 "The Belt and Road Initiative", Xinhua News Agency, https://www.researchgate.net/figure/The-Belt-and-Road-Initiative-Source-Xinhua-News-Agency_fig4_321689811

33 George Tsiagalakis, "Periplous of the Erythraen Sea map according to description from source text", Wikipedia, 26 December 2014, https://wikisource.org/wiki

34 "India participates in 20th ASEAN-India Economic Ministers' Meeting in Semarang, Indonesia", Ministry of Commerce and Industry, Press Information Bureau, Government of India, httpws://pib.gov.in/PressReleaseframePage.aspx?PRID=1950902#:~:text=I ndia% 20and%20ASEAN%20register ed%20a,global%20trade%20 in%202022%2D23

35 Saurabh Sharma, "77th Independence Day: Here's when India is likely to become the world's 3rd largest economy", Business Today, 14 August 2023, https://www.businesstoday.in/latest/story/77th-independence-day-heres-when-india-is-likely-to-become-the-worlds-3rd-largest-economy-394149-2023-08-14

36 "India will be a developed nation by 2047, its economic growth 'natural by-product' of 9 years stability: PM Modi", The Economic Times, 03 September 2023, whttps://m.economictimes.com/news/india/india-will-be-developed-nation-by-2047-its-economic-growth-natural-by-product-of-9-years-stability-pm-modi/articleshow/103324093.cms#

37 Duvvuri Subbarao, "So, Where Will We Be in 2047", The Times of India, 18 August, 2023, 22

38 "RBI Bulletin", Reserve Bank of India, 17 July 2023, https://www.lexite.com/eDocs/610.pdf

39 "The Ocean", OECD, https://www.oecd.org/ocean/topics/ocean-economy

40 Arvind Panagariya, "Dollar Today, Rupee Tomorrow", The Times of India, 21 August, 2023, 12

41 "Indian Shipping Statistics 2021", 04 July 2022, Ministry of Ports, Shipping and Waterways, https://shipmin.gov.in/sites/default/files/ISS_2021_FINAL.pdf

42 "India's Share of International Shipping", Ministry of Ports, Shipping and Waterways, 03 December 2021, https://pib.gov.in/PressReleaseselframePage.aspx?PRID=1777771

43 "Cabinet approves scheme for promotion of flagging of merchant ships in India by providing subsidy support to Indian shipping

companies in global tenders floated by Ministries and CPSEs", Ministry of Ports, Shipping and Waterways, 14 July 2021, https://pib.gov.in/PressReleasePage.aspx?PRID=1 735384#:~:text=b)%20 Currently%20the%20Indian%20fleet,7.8%25%20in%202018%2D19

44 Annual Report 2020-21, Government of India, Ministry of Ports, Shipping and Waterways, 13 August 2021, https://shipmin.gov.in/sites/default/files/AnnualReport2021_0.pdf

45 Mathew Rochat, "China's Growing Dominance in Maritime Shipping", The Diplomat, 18 December 2021, https://thediplomat.com/2021/12/chinas-growing-dominance- in-global-shipping

46 Compiled by the author from data in "Country Maritime Profiles", UNCTADstat, 20 October 2022, https://unctadstat.org/CountryProfile/en-GB/index.html

47 Wai Ming To and Peter K.C. Lee, "China's Maritime Economic Development: A Review, the Future Trend and Sustainability Implications", Sustainability, MDPI, 14 December 2018, https://mdpi-res.com/d_attachment/sustainability/sustainability-10-04844/article_deploy /sustainability-10-04844.pdf?version+1545190434#: ~:text=according%20to%20official%20data%20from,China %20 total%20gross %20domestic%20product

48 Yin Kedong, Zhe Liu, Caixia Zhang, Shan Huang, Junchao Li, Lingyun Lv, Xiaqing Su, Runchuan Zhang, "Analysis and forecast of marine economy development in China", Marine Economics and Management, Emerald Insight, ISSN: 2516-158X, 23 May 2022, https://www.emerald.com/insight/content /doi/10.1108/MAEM-10-2021-0009/full/html

49 Ibid, "Annual Report 2021-22", Ministry of Shipping, Ports and Waterways

50 Ibid, "Annual Report 2021-22", Ministry of Shipping, Ports & Waterways

51 "Maritime India Vision 2030", Ministry of Shipping, Ports & Waterways, Government of India, 12 February 2021, https://sagarmala.gov.in/sites/default/files/MIV%202030%Report.pdf

52 PM's Address at the Global Maritime India Summit 2023", PIB, 17 October 2023, https://pib.gov.in/PressReleaseframePage.aspx?PRID=1968335

53 Jude Blanchette et al,"Hidden Harbours – China's State-backed Shipping Industry", CSIS Briefs, CSIS, https://www.americanmaritime partnership.com/wp-content/uploads/2021/01/Hidden-Harbours_Brief_Final-1.pdf

54 "Economic Contribution of Indian Ports", Indian Economic Service, https://ies.gov.in/pdfs/ports-economic-Contribution.

55 Definition formulated by author.

Author

Vice Admiral AK Chawla, PVSM, AVSM, NM, VSM, superannuated from the Indian Navy on 30 November 2021 as the Flag Officer Commanding-in-Chief of the Navy's Southern Command. Over the course of his career, he has commanded five warships, including the aircraft carrier, INS *Viraat* and the Indian Navy's Western Fleet. He is an accomplished maritime thinker and author, and has completed his PhD on 'The Role of Maritime Power in China's Grand Strategy'. An active contributor to various defence journals, he is currently an Eminent Resource Faculty - Adjunct Professor for the Rashtriya Raksha University and a Council Member of the United Services Institute, as also several other think tanks, besides being involved in various social and environmental initiatives.